Stephen Colwell

The Five Cotton State and New York

Stephen Colwell

The Five Cotton State and New York

ISBN/EAN: 9783337416676

Printed in Europe, USA, Canada, Australia, Japan

Cover: Foto ©Suzi / pixelio.de

More available books at **www.hansebooks.com**

THE

FIVE COTTON STATES

AND

NEW YORK;

OR,

REMARKS

UPON THE

SOCIAL AND ECONOMICAL ASPECTS

OF THE

SOUTHERN POLITICAL CRISIS.

———————•———————

JANUARY, 1861.

THE

FIVE COTTON STATES

AND

NEW YORK.

THE CONSTITUTION OF THE UNITED STATES — BENEFITS OF A GENERAL GOVERNMENT.

THE Constitution of the United States has survived the wear and tear of three-quarters of a century. If it is now for the first time in serious danger, it is no small proof of its vitality and power. It has withstood the undermining processes of human folly: it has escaped from perils by factions fraught with villany and regardless of consequences; from perils by fraud, from perils by treason, and from perils by great and conflicting interests. The civilized world has been shaken to its foundations by changes and revolutions which have occurred since the birth of our government. Some of the most disastrous wars the world has ever witnessed have swept off millions upon millions of the human family. Mutual slaughter by civilized men has seldom, in the history of the world, accomplished greater destruction in the same time. Republics and thrones have sprung up and flourished in full-grown vigor for a few years, and then disappeared in a night. Our government has thus far successfully overcome all obstacles to its progress, and put to shame every voice that threatened its existence. It was never expected to escape all encounter with the perils to which every human institution is, soon or late, exposed. Human nature has, in

(3)

the last four-score years, exhibited the same tendency to
evil which stares upon us in every page of history; the
same readiness to pull up that which was planted, and
pull down that which was built; the same promptness to
seize the sword upon every occasion of quarrel; the same
grasping after our own interests; the same blindness
to the interests of others.   There has been no period of
the world in which the highest qualities of statesmanship
were more required.   We have had an encounter with one
of the most powerful nations of the world, and came off
creditably.   We invaded a neighboring nation, and sent
on that errand officers whose military skill and bravery
commanded the admiration of Europe; and soldiers direct
from the avocations of civil life, whose courage and endurance were worthy of the officers by whom they were
led.   We have had controversies of more or less importance with every power of Europe.   Through all this we
have risen to the rank of one of the great powers of the
world.   From thirteen States, with three millions, we
have grown to thirty-three States, with upwards of thirty
millions of inhabitants. 'Our progress in industry and
wealth is quite as remarkable as in dominion, and is, in
fact, admitted to have no parallel.

It is safe to assume that this extraordinary advance in
dominion, population, and wealth could never have been
made, but under the favoring circumstances of a uniform
policy, and continuous peace among the States: freedom
from war, and its devastations, could, however, only have
been secured by means such as the cohesive power of the
Constitution and laws of the United States.   But whilst
peace and uninterrupted industry have thus turned to good
account the unequalled natural advantages of our match-
less country, it may be very true, indeed it could not be
otherwise, than that any policy or system of legislation
uniform for such a wide extent of territory, for so great a
variety of interests, institutions and people, must in some
instances work injury or annoyance to a portion of the

people. Such has been the case in our confederacy. Some of the subjects upon which diversities of opinion have arisen are Direct Taxation, Internal Improvements, Slavery, Free Trade, Protection to Domestic Industry, and Protection to Foreign Commerce.

If such topics as these cannot, in this country, be discussed without limitation, and if decisions cannot be reached which should command the assent of all, the hope of maintaining free governments might as well be given up at once, for questions as important and serious must be met in every country; in point of fact, they have been met and discussed for eighty years, with the excitement of discussion not unfrequently at the highest pitch to which the interest felt in such subjects could carry it. We have hitherto passed through these scenes safely, and fully vindicated our capacity for self-government. So far as the questions involved are concerned, we can do so again. Although Slavery is one of these delicate topics, and involves questions the most difficult of solution, we do not hesitate to say that there is patriotism, forbearance, intelligence, and discrimination enough to meet and settle, wisely and well, every question to which that subject can give rise.

We do not mean to make light of this matter: far from it. It is one of the most momentous and interesting which can engage the minds and hearts of the people of this or any country; we only intend to say that it is susceptible of adjustment under our constitution in such manner, that States in which Slavery exists, and those in which it does not, can remain peaceably and honorably together under the same general government. It may be quite impossible to decide which of these two classes of States has most to answer for in the way of offences against the other, or to say whose bill of grievances as against the other is the heaviest. Each heart most feels its own bitterness, and each of these parties must be allowed to fill up and utter its own bill of complaint. They can never

be brought to think alike; but they can, if they please,
decide what is to be done, and draw a line beyond which
neither must go. The motives and interests which have
thus far held the States together are strong enough to hold
them together still, so far as Slavery is concerned. What
has already occurred, exaggerated by party spirit, should
not discourage prolonged efforts to heal present difficulties. Slavery, as protected by the Constitution of the
United States, has more friends in the Northern States
than it has in all the world beside—friends who would
march by the hundred thousand for its protection and defence as it exists under the Constitution.

GRIEVANCES — QUESTIONS OF THE POLITICAL CRISIS.

The real questions which now agitate the Southern
States, and which have shaken the fidelity and patriotism
of so many leading citizens of those States, are; — Where
is the political power of the country to be lodged? Who
is to wield its patronage? and, Where is its wealth to be
concentrated? These are the questions which give inten-
sity to the agitation, — to the words and actions of promi-
nent men in the South. It is no new thing, if the unex-
pressed motives in a political movement are more powerful
than those which are avowed. The under-current, which
sweeps backward from the shore, though unseen, has often
more power than the breakers which come thundering
over the surface with so much splash and display. It does
not appear to us a subject of legitimate complaint, that
Southern politicians enter upon such inquiries as those
just indicated. We do not think they need be kept in
the background. If our general government is destined
for a duration of ages, it must be able to encounter all the
questions which private and public interests, which ambi-
tion, bad passions and the complications of social and
political life, may offer. The very questions which between
isolated States can only be settled by arms, must be met

and settled between our States by resort to the intellectual and moral qualities of statesmanship. If our government is worth preserving for one reason more than another, it is that it may save the States from the calamity of war; and we cannot doubt that it has been efficient in saving us from many bloody and ruinous contests, in which the conflicting interests of the last eighty years would have precipitated us. One war of five years would destroy the fruits of twenty-five years' industry.

We propose to offer some remarks upon certain of the topics above suggested for the consideration of those whose discontent is so rapidly ripening into revolution. It may be assumed, we think, that no thought of secession would have been entertained but under motives of the strongest kind: the oppression which makes even the wise man mad, could alone have driven the men of South Carolina to the desperate measure of forsaking the constitution of the United States. What these powerful motives are may be gathered with considerable accuracy from the speeches, writings, and conversation of the leading politicians of that State. In her colonial days and at the time of the adoption of the Constitution of the United States, South Carolina stood in the front rank in point of wealth, education, and aristocratic style of living; she could have claimed high distinction in many other respects, in comparison with her sister colonies and States. The City of Charleston enjoyed a like distinction among the cities of North America, its inhabitants being in high repute for their intelligence, refinement, and liberal style of living. Although the people still preserve their high character individually, their State and city have fallen far behind many others in the race of population, wealth, and power. The City of Philadelphia has a population nearly equal to the whole State of South Carolina. The cities of New York and Brooklyn have together a population more than double that State. These are specimens of unfavorable comparisons suggested to the people of that State when they come to the North. Georgia and North Carolina have both outstripped the neighbor which lies between them ; and South Carolina has come to the conclusion that she is robbed by New York of that trade and wealth to which her favorable position entitles her.

That there is enough in this to arouse the attention of South Carolinians — to induce an inquiry into causes and a search for remedies, is quite true; but surely not enough, when added to all the grievances of that State in reference to Slavery, to justify a rush from the Union. Wise men count the cost of great undertakings ; prudent men look before they leap. The men of South Carolina do neither: they bolt from the Union and their allegiance with as much precipitation as from a house in flames. They put in imminent peril wives, children, property, Slavery itself, and the very constitution of the society in which they live, and which they profess to prize far above the Union : they dash headlong into perplexities and inconsistencies of law and administration, from which there is no retiring with dignity, and no advancing but with treason and dishonor. They have attained a position in which, on one hand, they have the ruin of industry and commerce, and on the other, civil war and ultimate humiliation. This is the work of insane passion. If secession is possible, it is so only by a tribunal constituted like that which formed the Union — by a convention capable of amending the constitution, or forming a new one. Firmness, deliberation, and wisdom might have carried such a measure. In the Union, South Carolina would be ever safe from border wars and their attendant evils, so specially dangerous to her : out of it, she is launched upon the sea of national hostilities, where the storms of war are inevitable. The effort to fight her battles in the Union has not been persevered in as the interests involved demanded. It is a lack of moral courage — it is mental cowardice to shrink from a contest for which our national institutions provide every needful arena.

THE COMMERCIAL POLICY OF THE UNITED STATES, AND SOUTHERN INTERESTS.

It is urged, we know and believed, that the commercial policy of the United States is injurious to Southern interests — so injurious as not to be endurable, and as far more than to counterbalance all the advantages of the Union. This has been long and earnestly asserted, and certainly deserves the most careful inquiry. We have for more than twenty-five years been devoted to the study of the industrial and commercial system of the United States, yet we could never see on what foundation this conclusion rested. We have often admired the intellect and the ingenuity brought to its support. The facts by which such positions can be demonstrated are not accessible in any system of commercial statistics within our reach, and the attempts at demonstration seem to omit elements indispensable to sound conclusions. Let us look at it a little, as connected with the production of Cotton, which is the item of Southern industry supposed to suffer most from this injurious policy.

The mode of disposing of their cotton is that which the planters themselves have adopted, uncontrolled by any national legislation. The expense consists, in transportation to the port whence it is shipped to Europe or to a Northern destination at home, the charges of shipping, freight to Europe, commissions on advances, and commissions on sales. Exchange is sometimes a profit, and sometimes a loss. The ports whence the cotton is shipped for a foreign market are, Charleston, Savannah, Mobile, and New Orleans — the latter receiving about one-half of the whole quantity. The management of the cotton at these cities is wholly under the control of the planters who have not previously sold their cotton, and their factors or agents, and is the best no doubt which their experience and commercial skill can devise. The planter either sells his cotton at once, and realizes the amount in the way which best suits him: he ships it northward, coastwise, and to Europe on his own account; or, having received advances on account, it is shipped in the name of the party who has made advances. For the amount shipped coastwise domestic bills are drawn, and for the most part sold or discounted in the cities where the cotton is first received. Against the amount shipped to Europe foreign bills are drawn, and sold wherever the best rate can be obtained for them, which is almost always at New York, because that is the great market of foreign exchange for the United States. It is there that the importers of foreign goods are concentrated, and thence their remittances are made. There the buyers of exchange congregate, and there, of course, the best price can be obtained; and that is the chief reason why the planter and his agents send their foreign bills to New York. Bills can be sold in that city when there is no demand elsewhere. A very large proportion of the money advanced upon cotton, at all the places of delivery, comes from New York; and bills drawn upon cotton are transmitted thither, to reimburse advances. Besides this, the merchants of the whole cotton region find it their advantage, as well as convenience, to pay for all their purchases at the North and their purchases abroad through New York: it is, therefore, a matter not only of convenience, but economy, to keep a large deposit in that city, where it is more available for the uses to which it is to be applied, than if in their own banks.

This vast business is carried on by the producers of cotton and their agents precisely in the way which experience teaches them to be most for their advantage. They are untrammelled by any Northern control but that which is of their own choice. These large transactions have fallen into the very channels, which the unrestrained action of those concerned have turned them; and this is in complete accordance with that system of political economy which is so earnestly and ably advocated by the orators and writers of Charleston. They maintain that trade should be entirely free, because men understand their own interests best, and should not be disturbed by the hand of government in their management. So far their theory and their mode of business run together, and the Free Trade principle is perfectly exemplified.

FOREIGN EXCHANGE.

But it is alleged that the foreign exchange of the South being all effected at New York, leaves a great profit there, which is so much abstracted from the Southern purse. There is no doubt that the business of Southern Exchange, that is, the converting bills drawn upon foreign countries for the value of cotton into money at home, is mainly effected at New York, for the simple reason that those who are concerned find it to their advantage, both in point of economy and convenience. The aggregate of profit thus made by New York is less than one per cent. on the amount of Southern bills purchased. It could not be done so satisfactorily to the parties interested, elsewhere in the United States, and it could not be done there at so low a rate, but for its concentration. If one hundred millions of dollars of Southern bills drawn on cotton are sold there annually, and that is probably the outside figure, it may leave, at the utmost, seven hundred and fifty thousand dollars of profit to the banks and dealers in exchange. If this business were withdrawn to the South from New York, it would be divided between Mobile, Savannah, Charleston, and New Orleans—one-half going to the latter city, and the remainder to the others, in proportion to their share of the business. In point of fact, these cities could not effect so large an amount of exchange, for they have neither the means nor the purchasers. It is well known that the parties who advance on cotton reimburse themselves through New York, or capital from there is employed directly in Southern ports to make such advances. If New York capital should be suddenly diverted from this channel of employment, it would have disastrous effects upon the interests of the Cotton States. Even if such a change were effected, it could not benefit the planter, who would have to pay others for the same service, and at a higher rate. Some banks and individuals in the Southern cities might profit; but as they could not for a long time extend the same facilities in the way of advances, the planters would suffer to an extent which could not be compensated by the increased profits of the bankers. This business of the exchange consequent upon the export of cotton, has assumed its present shape under the hands of those most interested in it; and it cannot be changed suddenly without great loss, suffering, and inconvenience to those who are concerned.

WHO PAYS THE DUTIES.

The grievance, however, which is most insisted upon by writers and speakers of the Cotton States is, that the heavy duties imposed by the United States bear with undue severity upon them; many do not hesitate to assert that they pay all, or nearly all, the revenue of our government derived from duties on foreign goods. That this is believed, is evinced by the reiteration of the statement. It is sometimes supported by the argument, that as the return for Southern cotton is wholly in foreign commodities, the duty imposed upon them is virtually a tax upon the Southern cotton. This position is specious enough to mislead those who do not trouble themselves to think or inquire. Those who do, easily detect the fallacy. The consumer of imported goods must pay not only the foreign cost, but the duties and all intervening profits and charges; the producers of cotton pay duties, under our system, only upon such goods as they consume. They either sell their cotton at home, or send it to a foreign market; and in either case they get the best price they

.can, and are paid in cash, or in such currency or credits as suits the purposes of the sellers and their agents. The funds thus obtained are managed and applied by the sellers of the cotton according to the exigencies of their business — the main part going, by an inexorable law of industry and trade, to defray the expenses of producing cotton and transporting it to the place of sale. The planters of cotton are, in this respect, situated as all other producers — they pay duties only according to their consumption of foreign goods, and are governed in their purchases by the price and quality, and their individual interests in the matter.

Those who go deeper into the subject do not rest their complaint upon this fallacy, but insist that all the goods consumed by them are affected by the heavy duties imposed — the domestic as well as the imported. It is alleged that the duties on foreign goods keep the prices of domestic products at the same level, thereby subjecting the cotton planter, who produces an article marketable abroad, to the necessity of paying increased rates for all his supplies. This opens a complicated subject, upon which, though much has been said and written, opinions are yet very diverse. The space to which we design to confine these remarks is not sufficient for such a topic; we pass it now, for the purpose of stating some facts which will enable us to present it in various points of view.

THE FIVE COTTON STATES.

It would be interesting, doubtless, to know whether an equal population, employing slave labor, paid more or less of the duties upon imported goods than that which does not employ it. By analyzing the entire expenditure of the five Cotton States of South Carolina, Georgia, Florida, Alabama, and Mississippi, we may ascertain, if not with certainty, yet with a fair approximation, what proportion of their income goes to the support of the government.

The States just named had, by the census of 1850, a white population of 1,565,554, which, estimating at the rate of increase between 1840 and 1850, has increased at the present time to 2,060,078. The slave population, estimating at the rate between 1840 and 1850, has swelled its numbers from 1,458,745, in 1850, to 2,187,322, in 1860, making the population of these five States, at the present time, 4,247,410.

It is frequently stated that the people of the Cotton States do not raise their own food. It is well known that the people of the five States to which we now refer are large purchasers of flour, pork, and other articles of food, the produce of other States; they are also sellers of food for man and beast. It may be, their sales in this particular are equivalent to their purchases. If not, they certainly transgress every sound principle of industrial economy, as the occupiers of such a soil in such a climate; and are inexcusable, if they pay the expense of transporting from elsewhere such articles of domestic provisions as they consume. We shall assume, for our purpose, that they do produce food for their own consumption, or, at least, that what they import is paid for by what they export. This leaves their great crop of cotton, and their manufactures, and the products of the mechanic arts, free of all incumbrance for food to meet other needful expenditure, and for accumulation as capital.

The cotton crop of these five States was, according to the census of 1850, eighty per cent. of the whole product of the United States, and if that proportion is maintained, may be stated at three millions two hundred thousand bales, yielding, at forty dollars per bale, the vast sum of $128,000,000.

THEIR EXPENDITURES — COST OF PRODUCTION — DUTIES.

We next inquire to what purposes the five great Cotton States apply their annual income. Having assumed that the same soil which produced the cotton has produced the food, the proceeds of their cotton and manufactures are applicable to other necessities of social life and Southern industry. By the census of 1850, the agricultural implements and machinery connected with planting in these States were stated to be of the value of $21,577,889. As the cotton crop has increased from two millions and a half to four millions in 1860, this value is now $40,000,000. This property is subject to constant deterioration by wear; its repair is a necessity constantly recurring, and, to a large extent, it is yearly replaced by improved implements, involving an expenditure of not less than fifteen per cent. on the entire value of this investment.

The annual expenditure for clothing the negroes, for overseeing, for medical attendance, and for other occasional but unavoidable expenses pertaining to the well-being of slaves, consumes a vast sum, which fifty millions will scarcely cover.

The expenses of packing cotton, transportation to port of shipment, shipping charges, commissions, foreign freight, interest, discount, and exchanges, are a heavy charge upon its production.

There are the further burdens of interest on mortgages of real estate, and payments on negroes purchased *;

---

* Estimating the number of negroes purchased by Alabama, Florida, Georgia, and Mississippi, at the rate by which the slaves in those States increased beyond the rate of increase of the whole slave population, we find they purchased, between 1840 and 1850, slaves to the number of 159,743, or 15,974 yearly; which, at the rate of $1000 each, drew every year from those States $15,974,000. South Carolina sold slaves in those ten years to the amount of $39,167,000.

which, together, must yearly absorb a large portion of the planter's income.

Besides this, it must be noted, that every producer of cotton has a large capital invested in land and negroes. His business should keep this capital unimpaired, besides furnishing an income sufficient for the maintenance of his family and that generous expenditure in which planters are accustomed to indulge — this must be left to the estimate of those who are considering the subject. The natural increase of the slaves is only three per cent. per annum.

A careful examination warrants us in stating the cost of making cotton and delivering it at the port of shipment, or in the markets of the United States, at not less, on the average of all places and soils in the five Cotton States, than $24 per bale. The cost of placing 3,200,000 bales in the ports of the South or markets of the North is not less than $76,800,000. This sum taken from $128,000,000, the price supposed to be realized, leaves for the producers a surplus of $51,200,000. If we take from this surplus the money used by the planters for purposes where money is indispensable — as, for taxes, payment of interest, purchase of negroes,—say one-half the surplus, or $25,600,000, which is only a small fraction over $12 for each white person, this would leave the same amount for the purchase of foreign goods and for the purchase of productions of Northern States.

This exhibit forbids the idea that the people of the five States pay as much or more than their proper proportion of the duties upon foreign goods. That proportion is two dollars for each head ; for our whole revenue by customs is about $60,000,000, for thirty millions of people. If the sum above specified as applicable to the purchase of American and foreign goods were all expended for the latter, it would make only one dollar per head for average duties. But the supposition is not allowable. These people, it is true, pay duties on so much cotton bagging and negro clothing as they import; but, according to the annual Treasury Reports on Commerce, that is a small amount. The value of cotton bagging imported is stated to have been $8,296 in the fiscal year ending July, 1858, and $14,067 the year previous. These Reports furnish no indications of heavy importations of articles suitable for negro clothing. There is no evidence, that we can find, showing that the planters pay as much as ten cents per head of the whole population for duty on cotton bagging and negro cloths, cotton or woollen. The supposition above made is not allowable, because it is well known that these Southern people are large purchasers of Northern productions. Some writers estimate this importation from the North as high as $150,000,000 *; at which rate the proportion of the five States would be $75,000,000. Deducting from this $20,000,000 (an amount already included in the cost of making cotton), expended in agricultural implements, machinery, &c., and we have $55,000,000; an amount which is too large to be purchased from the North, but upon prolonged credits, to go on accumulating as a debt, until discharged in the course of years by the combined contingencies of large crops and high prices.

From the climate occupied by the cotton planters, and their habit of residing in the country, and dressing in a plain and inexpensive manner whilst at home, it is believed they consume foreign goods, paying high duties, in great moderation. If the same people were residents of cities, their consumption of such goods would probably be three times greater. A simple inspection of the list of articles usually imported demonstrates that they are not wanted at the South in the large quantities required at the North, such as wool, woollen goods, iron and steel, furs, and various raw materials of manufactures. The Southern people are then exempt,

* Southern Wealth and Northern Profits. By T. P. Kettell. New York, 1860.

2

by their habits of life, by the nature of their industry, and by the fact of half their whole population being slaves, from their full proportion of the burden of the customs. That is their advantage, and not their misfortune, if, as they allege, their system of industry is the best.

We cannot decide what proportion of the surplus of $25,600,000 above mentioned is expended in foreign, and what in Northern domestic goods; but we have no doubt that much the largest share goes for Northern commodities, and therefore assign $15,600,000 to the latter, and $10,000,000 to the former. The average duty on the latter is eighteen per cent., and the whole duty paid $1,800,000 — less than fifty cents a head of the whole population.

From all the evidence and statistics to which we have access, we are at a loss to detect any proof that the population of the five Cotton States pay in duties directly, one dollar for each person. It is possible they make up the amount of two dollars each by increased prices on domestic commodities. But as the whole population of the United States pay two dollars direct duties on the average, they must of course pay their portion of the indirect duties. There does not then appear to be any substantial ground of complaint in this respect.

ARE GREAT QUESTIONS TO BE SOLVED BY INTELLECT OR BY FORCE OF ARMS?

It is the subject of frequent and strong complaint, on the part of the South, that the present course of business in the United States is extremely unfavorable, if not unjust, to the South, especially to the five States of South Carolina, Georgia, Florida, Alabama, and Mississippi. It is assumed, by those who urge this grievance, that New York absorbs a very large and undue share of the trade which properly belongs to Southern cities and Southern merchants. This presents an important inquiry, which

well deserves the study of Southern and Northern states-
men and political economists. We have at various times,
for more than thirty years, given earnest attention to it,
and have endeavored to comprehend the questions of
social economy which were rising between States and
people North, and States and people South, in our rapidly
and widely-extending country. In a territory so large,
embracing climates and productions so varied, it could not
be otherwise than that questions would arise, new, com
plicated, and presenting special difficulties, from the magnitude of the interests involved, and the novelty of the
institutions under which they were to be settled. Questions which, in the past history of the world, were adjusted
by long and devious efforts of diplomacy, backed by the
plain and easily understood arguments of hundreds of
thousands of men in arms, and not unfrequently by the
actual arbitrament of battles, are among us for the first
time on such a scale, to be settled by legislators, and
judges, and elective magistrates. At this moment there
is a political tempest raging in the United States — a
mighty rush of excited feelings and clashing opinions,
roused by real events, and bearing on subjects of real importance. Such feelings and opinions, lashed into madness by the unscrupulous doings and statements of political
partizans, would have thrust us into an embittered war
ere now under any other institutions. They have kept us
thus far from bloodshed; they will conduct us through
this national crisis, if we, as a people, prove ourselves
worthy of our political privileges and experience.

As a whole people, we must learn to realize our new
and exalted position —we must rise intellectually to appreciate new problems and aspects of statesmanship, legislation, and social economy. As we increase in wealth,
power, and population, our wisdom should increase.
Above all, we must increase in patience, forbearance, and
in that knowledge of human nature which will teach us
that no question can arise among us, as a people or as

States, which cannot be more wisely settled, under our institutions, than by any possible method outside of them. We must not forget that the teachings of the old world, where standing armies are in the background of all political and economical agitations and disputes, do not, and should not apply here. It is very possible we may not agree, but we should be able to understand each other, and find the true point of mutual concession and adjustment; and no effort should be regarded as too great or onerous, and no time too long, where the alternative was disunion and civil war.

Among the difficult questions which must be met are those which arise from different industrial and social systems existing in States far apart. Let it then be our effort to settle these not for ourselves only, but for all the world. Elsewhere they are settled by armies and navies — let us be the first to settle them by the weapons of intellect, knowledge, and social skill. In this mode of adjustment let us show, in time to come, as we might have shown in times past, that we have no superiors in the world; let us exemplify that this mode of adjustment demands the highest grade of mind, the largest knowledge of the world, and the heroism of moral courage.

COMMERCE: WHAT IS IT?

Before entering on the subject of the Southern complaint, that the North has unduly absorbed the trade and business of the South, we wish to make a remark or two on the subject of commerce, as to which there is a fallacy resting in many minds, which it is worth while to try to remove. When two persons, with each a commodity in hand, give one for the other, that is an act of commerce; and although the exchange may be for the advantage of both, no addition has been made to the wealth of the community in which they live. This is just as true of two nations as of two individuals. The industry which increases the whole quantity of commodities is that which creates wealth. Commerce does not add to the stock of commodities—it distributes the stock which exists. When two persons exchange as we have just supposed, there is no expense attending the transaction, and therefore no tax upon the exchange. But to carry on commerce in the mode needful for the accommodation of civilized communities, great expense is incurred. Commerce collects, transports, stores, assorts, distributes, and sells wholesale and retail; and for these purposes it requires merchants, warehouses, stores, ships, canals, railways, money, and innumerable other agencies, all of which are an expense to productive industry. Commerce never makes a bale of cotton, a yard of cloth, or a pound of iron. Undoubtedly, it stimulates and promotes production, because production could not go on without distribution, and because the capital accumulated becomes a powerful assistant to industry. But the whole of the agencies of commerce are, nevertheless, an expense and a tax upon productive labor. We should endeavor, by all proper agencies, to increase production; but the effort should be as constant to dispense with such agencies of commerce as may be no longer required for the special purposes of distribution.

There is no doubt that these distributing agents, the merchants, from their intermediate position between the maker and the consumer, between the seller and the buyer, obtain an immense advantage by the knowledge they acquire of the position and necessities of all classes of society, which they turn to such profitable account, that, from being agents of industry, they become masters and merchant princes — from intermediates they become principals. They absorb a portion of the profits which in strictness belongs to the producers, and not the distributors of wealth. Where industry is left to the free manipulation of merchants, and no special care is taken of the producers, that result is inevitable.

THE FIVE COTTON STATES AND THEIR PRODUCTIONS.

The five States mentioned produce 3,200,000 bales of cotton, worth say $128,000,000 ; but the expense of the commercial agencies through which this cotton passes amounts, including transportation, freights, commissions, &c., to five dollars per bale. This is a heavy tax, now paid by cotton planters to commerce. It has always been and is now a legitimate inquiry, whether this business can be done at less expense to the producer of cotton. The business has found its present channels and taken its present shape by the free choice of those concerned in it. So far as it has taken form in this country, it is the off-spring of the most perfect free trade in the world. The benefits of this trade, that is, the enjoyment of the $16,000,000 it yields, now belongs mainly to Charleston, Savannah, Mobile, New Orleans, New York, and Liverpool; but many other interests, such as railways, canals, ships, and steamers, partake largely. Now, if this business, so far as this country is concerned, could be concentrated at Charleston, Savannah, or Mobile, it might considerably promote the growth of those cities; but would the business be done at any less cost than at present? Would it benefit the producer, or strengthen his hands? Charleston, Savannah, Mobile, and New Orleans, are interested to draw from New York as many of the agencies and profits as they can ; but it does not so much concern the individuals who furnish the cotton which is the object of this trade. Those cities might, in a time of excitement, think it worth while to go out of the Union for the sake of the profit on the cotton trade; but the planters who produce the cotton have no interest in following them, as they can never have a government which will prove less expensive to them than that of the United States.

The idea now pretty extensively entertained in the South, that New York is fattening on Southern trade and business, is an utter delusion : New York is not piling up "Northern profits on Southern wealth." It is a misconception, which no unprejudiced man can entertain, if he will take the trouble to examine. Last year the outward shipments of cotton were,

From New York	156,911	bales.
" Charleston	326,500	"
" Savannah	259,179	"
" Mobile	478,606	"
" New Orleans	1,658,317	"

It is not, then, by the export trade in cotton that New York builds those avenues of princely mansions, which so much excite the notice of King Cotton's subjects in Charleston.

NEW YORK BUSINESS IN COTTON COMPARED WITH THE WHOLE BUSINESS OF THAT CITY.

Let us ascertain now, how much New York actually realizes by the cotton business. The cotton merchants in the Southern cities make advances on cotton, and probably charge two and a half per cent. on the value of the quantity exported. Last year this amounted to $131,000,000, of which they may have allowed

New York one and a quarter per cent........................	$1,637,500
Add for exchange on the whole, a half per cent.........	655,000
Add $5 per bale on 156,911 bales shipped from N. Y....	784,555
Let us suppose that New York makes ten per cent. on $131,000,000 worth of merchandise purchased with the proceeds of this export of cotton	13,100,000
	$16,177,055

This last item, $13,100,000, is more than double what it should be, if the author of "Southern Wealth and Northern Profits" approximates the truth in estimating the South to be the purchaser of $150,000,000 of Northern products yearly. We do not believe that the profits of New York, in all the transactions relating to raw cotton, exceed nine millions yearly; but we leave it as above. The contrast of the larger sum with the actual daily transactions of New York, the amounts of which are accurately known, will be strong enough.

The Banks of New York settle their claims against each other every day. These claims arise chiefly on notes discounted by them, or deposited with them for collection, and paid by checks on other banks than the one holding them. They include also the exchange of bank notes. These settlements amounted, in

1857, to a daily average of.......	$26,968,371.
1858, " " "	......	15,393,735.
1859, " " "	......	20,867,333.
1860, " " " ·	about	25,000,000.

The balances on these settlements, paid in specie, amounted to over one million of dollars daily. These adjustments do not include the payments made in the several banks by checks drawn on them by their own depositors, which may amount to $5,000,000 more, and they do not include the immense payments going on daily in New York out of bank. The entire value of the whole cotton crop of the United States rated at four millions of bales, and, at forty dollars a bale, worth $160,000,000, would equal only six or eight days' payments at the Clearing House of New York, and probably not six days' payments of the whole city.

It is often urged that New York enjoys an immense advantage in the use of Southern capital deposited in her banks. New York is, doubtless, the financial capital of the United States, and, as such, is the bank of the bankers of the whole country, who find it for their benefit to keep large deposits in that city. There is no doubt that the South derives great advantage from this commercial practice, and greater benefit from such amount of her funds as are deposited there, than if they were scattered in different banks at home. The concentration of money in New York furnishes to the South a far greater sum, at many times in the year, than the South ever has on deposit at one time. The deposit of Southern funds in New York is a purely financial expedient for the benefit of those who make the deposit. London and Paris are, financially, to their respective countries, what New York is to the United States.

We might make comparisons with the daily payments of Boston, Philadelphia, and Baltimore, to show how immensely the business transactions of each exceed what the whole amount of the cotton crop would make them, if they were dependent on that alone. But we think it will be more instructive to compare the five Cotton States of Alabama, Florida, Georgia, Mississippi, and South Carolina, with the eight States around New York, containing a little more than half the number of square miles, for the purpose of showing what is, much more than cotton, the real basis of the growth and wealth of that magnificent city. These five States cover 244,531 square miles, and contain a population of 4,247,410 inhabitants, of whom 2,060,078 are white. Their production of cotton is estimated at eighty per cent. of the whole crop, stated as above at 3,200,000 bales, worth $128,000,000 —which sum, apportioned among the whole population, gives $30 for each; if among the white population, it gives $82 to each person. We have conceded what many deny, that the food consumed by this whole population is produced by themselves, though its money value is far below the average cost of food in the Middle and Northern States. Food is, to a very large extent, produced by the planters, and consumed on the spot, and enters but to a limited extent the channels of trade. This is economy to the planter, and, in fact, indicates his true policy. At the valuation put, in the South, on the food they consume, it would not probably amount to $30 each; but as it would cost $50 if purchased as Northern people purchase their food, we put the production of these five States at $50 per head for their food, making $212,370,500. Of this large production, not more than ten per cent., or twenty millions, pays a dollar of profit to the trader or transporter. Not less than $20,000,000 per annum are thus saved. It is true, the sum thus saved would go far to sustain a middle class of traders and mechanics sufficient to double the populations of the cities and towns of these States; but Southern people differ upon the point whether such a population would be an advantage to their institutions and to their state of society.

MARYLAND, DELAWARE, PENNSYLVANIA, NEW JERSEY, NEW YORK, RHODE ISLAND, CONNECTICUT, MASSACHUSETTS, AND THEIR PRODUCTIONS.

The States of Maryland, Delaware, Pennsylvania, New Jersey, New York, Rhode Island, Connecticut, and Massachusetts cover 128,344 square miles, and contain a population, according to the census of 1850, of 8,036,152, which, by this time, has increased to above ten millions. The largest of these States, and the largest proportion of the people, are agricultural, and therefore it is safe to say, however much more enters into their trade, they produce their own food, so far as it is domestic, at a cost of $50 for each individual. Fully one-third of these ten millions reside in cities and towns, and purchase their food from hand to mouth, paying the highest retail price. The population being ten millions, and paying $50 each on the average for their food, yearly expend thus $500,000,000; and such is the traffic in provisions and breadstuffs in these States, that at least twenty-five per cent. on this sum goes into the hands of merchants, small traders, and other intermediate dealers and transporters. The large sum of $125,000,000 thus enures to their support, whose office is merely that of distributing sustenance to the people. It

is safe to say that two-fifths of this business, $200,000,000
at the least, is managed and controlled by New York merchants, or their agents, and that it affords a profit to the
large and small dealers of that city of twenty per cent. on
the whole amount, say $40,000,000.

The products of industry in those eight States, not pertaining to the food of man or beast, is stated, in the census
of 1850, at $687,828,248. Whatever doubts may be enter-
tained of the figures of that census, the magnitude of this
production is proved to be fully equal to this statement,
if not considerably beyond it, by the census of the State
of Massachusetts and that of New York, and by the various
estimates of Boards of Trade in many cities, proving that
the national census had fallen short of, instead of exceeding, the sum of industry in those States. The increase of
production in Massachusetts and New York, as shown by
the census of 1855 in each State, satisfies us that the estimate of fifty per cent. as the increase of production from
1850 to 1860, is not too large. We therefore give the
above sum with the addition of fifty per cent., viz.,
$1,031,742,372, as the product of the machinery, the
mines, and the mechanic arts, with the labor of those eight
States at this time. As the sales of these products have
their special centre in New York as a chief distributing
point, not less than $400,000,000 in value of these products
pay tribute to New York merchants, or to capital wielded
by them, in the shape of expenses, charges, and profits, of
not less than fifteen per cent., or $60,000,000, on sales
wholesale and retail.

It appears, then, from this approximation, that the five
Cotton States contribute to New York a business of two
hundred millions, yielding a profit of sixteen and a half
millions; and that the eight States neighboring to New
York furnish a business of six hundred millions, with a
profit of one hundred millions.

These two groups of States contain less than half the
population of the United States. It is well known that

the Western and South-western States are productive in a
high degree, and that they carry on a much heavier trade
with New York than the five Cotton States of which we
have spoken. We shall not err greatly, if we estimate
that the remaining States, with their sixteen millions of
population, furnish to New York as large a business, with
as much advantage in the way of profit, as the eight
specified. If we do not err in this, New York enjoys a
business of fourteen hundred millions of dollars, of which
two hundred come from the five Cotton States. If the
whole of the charges and profits be taken into account,
so far as they enure to New York, including freights, the
income resulting to that city on that business exceeds two
hundred and eighty millions of dollars — a sum far greater
than the gross value of the whole cotton crop of the United
States, and double the gross value of the cotton crop of the
five States.

These figures and statements ought to convince those
who have thought that the trade in products of Southern
industry was that which chiefly enriched and built up the
great cities of New York and Brooklyn, that they have
been laboring under a grievous mistake. The annual
profits of the business done in those cities far exceed the
gross product of Southern industry, leaving out of the
latter breadstuffs and provisions. To show that we have
not overrated the business of New York, we again refer
to the amount of the payments made there, of which we
have accurate returns from the Clearing House. These
reports show that the payments of the years specified were
as follows : —

1854	$5,750,455,987
1855	5,362,912,098
1856	6,906,213,328
1857	8,333,226,718
1858	4,756,664,386
1859	6,448,005,956
1860	7,231,143,056

(These years commence with October and end in September.

To this vast aggregate of payments one-third may be added for such as are not made through the Clearing House.

Almost every article in the channels of trade is sold more than once, and very many five or six or more times. Each of these sales may originate paper, which is collected through the banks; thus swelling the volume of payments above the mere value of the commodities which are being distributed. If, then, the commodities which are received into and distributed by New York are worth only fourteen hundred millions yearly, the amount of payments arising out of this business will be greatly increased by repeated transactions in the same articles. The payments are also largely increased in amount by operations in credit, money, and stocks. Thus the payments are swelled to the vast sum of eight or ten thousand millions in a year, upon all which New York gathers more or less profit. This furnishes to the South no real cause of complaint, and is, in fact, no injury. Philadelphia suffers more, far more, from this aggregation of business in New York than the whole State of South Carolina. It is all the legitimate and direct result of free trade between the States.

This great industry of the Northern, Middle, and Western States, not only builds up New York and Brooklyn, but also Boston, Philadelphia, Baltimore, Pittsburg, Cincinnatti, Louisville, St. Louis, Chicago, and a host of other cities, containing together a population and wealth double that of New York and Brooklyn. Cities do not thrive well upon Southern soil. There is no middle class to build and inhabit them; and no employment for such a class. There is no machinery for them to construct and keep in motion; there is no field for invention; few, if any, houses or factories to build; and, of course, the class of people who do this work cannot dwell in a country where the system of industry excludes them — where, in fact, they are not only not wanted, but repelled. The capitalists of the South believe that their interests are best promoted by exporting cotton, and importing the articles which this middle class would manufacture, while they were fed upon products of Southern soil, furnished with little addition to the force now employed in agriculture. A middle class of manufacturers and mechanics spread over the immense area of Southern territory, to the number of four millions, would consume of Southern products fifty dollars' worth each, and afford a market for two hundred millions of dollars' worth of breadstuffs and provisions, double the price of all the land in cultivation and the population of all the cities.

But if this middle class cannot safely be introduced into the system of Southern industry, then the effort should be made to train the slaves, as far as practicable, to the occupations of this middle class. It is, undoubtedly, possible to recast the industry of the South, so as to double its productiveness, with the same kind of labor, by introducing somewhat more skill, enterprise, and invention. Within thirty or forty years the agriculture of Great Britain has been revolutionized, and its products nearly doubled. The simple fact, that from five to eight times as much animal food can be raised under ground as above it, has become there an element of agriculture, has made every farm a manufactory of manure, and has attracted to farming, as a profitable business, men of science, of large capital and great enterprise. When the crops which develop under the ground, as well as those above it — when the fruits of the garden and orchard, are allowed their proper position in Southern agriculture, a new career of Southern production will begin, similar to that which has occurred in Great Britain.

It is a fact, worthy not only of remark, but of deep study, that the various systems of industry and of domestic trade prevailing in the United States, have been adopted, and long carried on, without any restriction between ourselves. Climate, soil, social institutions, natural character, and the free action of a people spread over a space much larger

than many of the largest countries of Europe, taken
together, have determined the kind and the localities of
our various branches of industry, and the position and
growth of our cities. This division of labor has formed
the channels of a domestic trade which has no parallel in
the world, for extent and value, among an equal number
of people. There is no other equal population, where the
actual producers — the planters, the farmers, the manufacturers and mechanics — pay so large a proportion of their
earnings to the intermediate classes, whose business it is
to distribute the products of industry. It seems to be
a heavy burden upon industry; but it is all the result of
individual choice and free trade in business. So far as
individuals, acting freely, can shape and consolidate a
great national industry, and domestic trade to correspond,
it has been done in this country. It is true, that in an
early period of our history the New England States, which
had betaken themselves to foreign commerce and the
shipping business generally, were driven from trade to
manufacturing by the non-intercourse acts and the following war with Great Britain. These States occupy a soil
and climate which permit no delay or hesitation in the
choice of employments. The people must work or starve.
. The Middle States betook themselves to agriculture, for
which their soil and habits were adapted; but, not finding
in New England nor abroad a market for their products,
they too began to manufacture, that they might establish
a population at their own doors to consume products of
their farms for which they could find no other market.
Both New England and the Middle States have, at vast
expense in the way of experiment, with large losses in a
struggle against foreign competition, and with an outlay
of ingenuity and invention previously without parallel,
succeeded, as a manufacturing people, beyond all antici-
pation. We have now a population of fifteen millions,
as well clad and with dwellings as well furnished as any
equal number of people; whose expenditure for clothing,

furniture, &c., may be safely estimated at fifty dollars a head — not including articles of domestic food; and yet of this production we receive from foreign countries less than ten dollars' worth for each person. We make at home more than four-fifths of our whole consumption, and we are the most lavish consumers in the world.

This aptness for manufacturing industry, and the permanent success which has at length been attained, have produced results unfavorable to a proper development of Southern and Western industry. The Southern States, having no shelter from the flood of Northern products, owing to the whole power of commercial regulation being lodged in Congress, were overwhelmed with every article required for their houses and plantations, to such extent, as to discourage all attempts at competition with an industry so supported by machinery, and so fortified by patents. The cheapness of the commodities thus furnished did not atone for the evil of their abundance, which effectually prevented that diversity of occupation essential to a sound and strong community, and an independent state of society. It prevented the due increase of the white population, and the growth of towns and cities. There could be no employment for such increase; the older States have therefore sent off their increase of population to other States. If South Carolina were to call home all her native-born citizens who reside out of the State, she would more than double her white population; but she would call them home to starve, unless a different system of industry were inaugurated.

If the Southern States had enjoyed the same unrestricted and untaxed intercourse with the rest of the world as this with the Northern States, the result could have been no better. Foreign merchants and manufacturers are as much given to crowding the markets to which they have free access, as those of our own country. In fact, if such had been the case, not a factory could have been built in the face of such competition as European merchants and manufacturers would have brought to the free ports of the South. The white population would have shrunk still more from a struggle in which neither skill, nor enterprise, nor capital in the South, could have thrown a shuttle, or lifted a hammer. The population would have, of necessity, become proportioned to the power to own slaves, and to the market for cotton. No white population would have been required, but the proprietors of the slaves, the overseers, and a few assistants; and to this condition society would have subsided in the States where the lands were occupied, or partly worn out, if the Southern ports had been open to the world without duty or restriction. Under such a policy there would have been even less diversity of occupation than has occurred under Northern competition. Something has been done, though far short of what the true interests of the Southern people demanded, under the protection of higher prices prevailing at the North, owing to the higher wages paid for labor in this country, and to the fact that our public revenue was derived from duties upon imports, with some discrimination in favor of domestic manufactures. Even with this aid the Northern and Middle States have incurred losses frightful to contemplate, in attaining to their present measure of success in manufactures.

As a revenue adequate to the purposes of government must, in some form, be paid under any circumstances, we cannot see what signal benefit could have accrued to the Southern people as a compensation for the utter repression of all production but that of cotton. They have had enough of that mistaken policy to create some doubts of its correctness.

It is a great mistake to suppose that the South could, by free ports, derive a benefit proportioned to the amount of duties now assessed upon foreign goods paid for by exported cotton. The expenses of making cotton are very largely made up of items which do not involve the consumption of imported goods. The interest on investments

3

in land and negroes, the purchase and keeping of mules, oxen, horses, agricultural implements and machinery, the replacing, repairing, and overseeing, the hospital expenses and medical attendance, the repairs to buildings, taxes, lumber, transportation to market, commissions, etc.:—all these, and other expenses which cannot be estimated at less than fifty per cent. on the value of the crop at the ordinary prices, are little affected by the duties paid at the Custom-House.

The planter of cotton could not pay this portion of the expense with foreign goods imported free of duty; it must, in the main, be paid in cash; and it is, to a large extent, done by receiving advances on cotton from the merchants to whom it is consigned, who in turn reimburse themselves by selling bills drawn on the cotton in New York, or elsewhere. The planters cannot save the amount of the duties on the value of the cotton exported, because they cannot afford to receive the whole value in foreign goods; the cotton exported is mortgaged for much more than half its value to pay debts and advances; it is exported for other account than that of the producers.

"TRACT No. 3"—DOCTRINES OF THE REVOLUTIONISTS.

Before dismissing this part of our subject, we take up a pamphlet now lying before us, published at Charleston in 1860, being "Tract No. 3. To the People of the South. Senator Hammond and the Tribune. By Troup. Read and send to your Neighbor." From the manner in which this production is put forth, we may take for granted it expresses the opinions of the men who are leaders of the present movement in Charleston. It would be very hard else to believe that Senator Hammond ever uttered what is there ascribed to him. The language quoted is from his speech in the Senate of the United States on the 4th of March, 1858, and consists chiefly of an eulogy upon the South. Upon the military power of the South it contains statements so marvellous, as to excite some wonder as to the extraor-

dinary things which are to be revealed in other depart-
ments of the concerns of that State. He has nothing to
say against the men of the North: "But they produce no
great staples that the South does not produce, while we
produce two or three, and those the very greatest, that she
can never produce." It is virtually denied here that our
manufacturers produce any staple goods, or that there can
be any other staples than those which are agricultural.
But even if that were the case, much might be advanced
in refutation of this position. Every Northern man will
smile at the extreme self-complacency which dictated such
an assertion. We shall only oppose to it the Northern
staple which is of cash value equal to the whole cotton
crop. We know it is objected to this, that hay, instead
of being a profitable crop, is a burden to the industry of
the North; that the South does not need such provender;
and that, to dispense with it, is a clear saving. The man who
invented this reply to the Northern boast about the hay
crop, thought he had rescued the South from the sad pre-
dicament of being outbragged. But as the Northern
farmers continue to produce and enlarge their crop of
hay, to sell it, and to put the money in their pockets, they
probably were never even struck with the plausibility of
the economical position which marks down the whole hay
crop to less than nothing. This wholesale depreciation
goes upon the principle that nothing is of any value unless
it is wanted at the South. There is a degree of self-complacency in this which approaches the superlative. Our
warm houses, our warm clothes, our coal, our multitu-
dinous machinery, our ships — but we need not specify;
we have, in the North, hundreds of millions invested in
property which is not wanted by the South; we produce
annually, of articles not wanted by the South, a value
many times that of the cotton crop — articles which are as
much cash articles as cotton.
    The Northern and Middle States produced, in 1850, up-
wards of eleven millions tons of hay, and they produce now

at least sixteen millions of tons, worth over two hundred millions of dollars in money. Northern hay is a very nutritious provender for horses and cattle, as is shown by the size and condition of the animals which are fed upon it. In the North, cattle are grown, by its help, to the common weight of 1000 to 1500 pounds; whilst those fed upon Southern pastures seldom exceed a third of that weight. The Southern people are, however, far from being insensible to the value of Northern hay, as any observing person will have seen who has been on the wharves, or in the stables of Southern cities, where it sells at a price which would carry the value of the whole crop of the North far above three hundred millions of dollars.*

---

* The following communication, which appeared in the Charleston Mercury, November 15th, 1860, furnishes a suitable commentary upon what is advanced above :

"NORTHERN HAY."

To the Editor of the Charleston Mercury :

We have habituated ourselves to dependence on the North for many things which might be produced at home. Any interruption of our intercourse with Northern ports will be attended with temporary inconvenience. For my part I desire this interruption, for it will set the seal to our deliverance from thraldom, and turn our attention to new and more profitable relations springing from free trade, untrammelled by political influences.

The point I would call attention to may seem a small matter; but almost every horse in Charleston, and many in some of the towns in the interior, is fed on Northern hay. Should the supply be cut off, we will feel the want severely. Moreover, should there arise any occasion for assembling or moving troops, especially on the seaboard, during this winter, we will find our operations cramped by this want sooner than by any other.

I would suggest, therefore, to rice-planters on all the rivers, that although straw is a poor substitute for hay, still it is a substitute, and an exceedingly cheap one. By selecting the best, that is, the greenest straw, and preserving and baling it as soon as threshed, it is

The strange notion which seems to have entered the minds of some of the Southern people, that no product of industry is to be regarded as an item of wealth, unless it is an article of export, is so absurd as scarce to deserve a denial, much less a formal refutation. The fact that the products of industry amount annually, in the United States, to upwards of three thousand millions of dollars, and that not more than ten per cent. of the amount is exported, is enough to dispel that fancy.

"But the strength of a nation depends, in a great measure, upon its wealth, and the wealth of a nation, like that of a man, is to be estimated by its surplus production. You may go to your trashy census-books, full of falsehood and nonsense — . . . you may estimate what is made throughout the country from these census-books; but it is no matter how much is made, if it is all consumed. If a man is worth millions of dollars, and consumes his income, is he rich? Is he competent to embark in any new enterprises? Can he build ships or roads? And could a people in that condition build ships or roads, or go to war? All the enterprises of peace and war depend upon the surplus productions of a people." The doctrine of surplus, as thus stated by Senator Hammond, will be new to men versed in the affairs of the world; but it was, no doubt, intended chiefly for the people of his own State, and to them it must have carried no small consolation. The idea of a surplus, as generally entertained in the North, whether of manufactures or of agriculture, is, what is left after paying expenses. The maker of cotton goods counts as his surplus that which remains to him at the end of the year, after paying for raw material, labor, and other unavoidable charges upon his production. The

at once in a shape to be portable, and to keep without deterioration. There is at least one kind of hay-press which is both efficient and cheap, costing less than $50; and at this crisis it may prove profitable to the planter, and useful to the State.   G. M.

word is used in another sense by the manufacturer who at the end of the year has not used all the raw material purchased for the supply of his establishment. He has a surplus; that is, it is in his possession or under his control. It is available for the next year. If a cotton planter were to sell his cotton, as soon as prepared for market, until he had realized the cost of making his whole crop, what remained would be his surplus, or, translated into plain Anglo-Saxon, it would be so much over and above expenses. This is the way men of business understand it; but the South Carolina Senator, certainly, propounds a doctrine far more consolatory to the people of that State. He announces, that whatever products his State exports to foreign countries or to the North is surplus. As the manufacturers of that State use no more cotton than would be grown upon two or three plantations, his doctrine is, that all the cotton made, with this small exception, is surplus and evidence of the wealth of the State; and this in the face of the fact, that it costs at least six cents a pound to make, and that nearly all the cotton is either sold or under heavy advances when it is exported. It is very safe to say, that nine-tenths of the cotton is exported on Northern or foreign account or under advances to three-fourths of its value. It is not exported by the planters nor by Southern merchants: it is sold or pledged, and then shipped for account of the purchaser or whoever makes the advances.

The Senator goes on to state, that in the year 1857 the foreign exports of the United States amounted to $279,000,000, and that "of this $158,000,000 were of the clear produce of the South." He then proceeds, by a process of quoting quite as questionable as consulting the "trashy census-books," to swell the amount of Southern exports to $220,000,000. Upon this summit of production he rests the claims of the supremacy of Southern industry and wealth. "The recorded exports of the South are now greater than the whole exports of the United States for

the last twelve years." . . . "If I am right in my calcu-
lations as to $220,000,000 of surplus produce, there is not
a nation on the face of the earth, with any numerous population, that can compete with us in produce *per capita*. It
amounts to $16.66 per head, supposing we have twelve
millions of people. England," he proceeds, "with all her
accumulated wealth, &c., makes but $16 of surplus pro-
duction per head"; and then he puts the North down to
ten dollars per head. According to this mode of estimating wealth, if South Carolina manufactured all her own
cotton, she would have no surplus production whatever:
the planter who sells his cotton to one of the Southern
factories, and gets the money for it, has no surplus, and
has not added to his own or the wealth of the State, because he has not exported his cotton.

If England were to build her factories in the South,
purchase and pay for all the cotton, and manufacture it
there, we cannot perceive how the Cotton States would
be any poorer; but upon the doctrine of the Senator of
South Carolina they would have lost all their surplus,
which by his rule is all their crop. But we need not
chase further this extraordinary assertion of the Senator;
it would not have been worthy of a moment's notice, but
for the fact that many in the South seemed to have been
inoculated with the same error, and are now suffering
severely in consequence. There is absolutely nothing in
the industry of the South, nothing in the character of the
people, nothing in the institution of slavery, nothing in
the skill, enterprise, or science of the people, which ex-
empts them individually or collectively from a law of
social economy, which applies to every system of production :—It matters not, whether the product be sold on
the spot where it is made, in the neighboring town or sea-
port, or whether it be sent round the world for a market;
what the commodity cost the producer in labor or money,
when compared with what the sale brings, clear of all
expenses, is the profit, surplus, or gain of the producer.

A large export trade in cotton might be carried on, in which the amount might run up to hundreds of millions, with a heavy loss every year. The question must still be with the South, as well as the North, what is left after the year's business is adjusted — that is, the surplus which will add to the common wealth.

Another of the Senator's axioms of political economy is, that a man may be worth millions, but he cannot be rich if he consumes his income. He applies this to the North, and on the ground that the North does not export its products, he concludes that, no matter how much is produced, it is all consumed. The condition of the North is, in the Senator's estimation, that it consumes its wealth, and has not, therefore, the ability "to build ships, or railroads, or embark in any new enterprise." Facts not very remote seem to contradict this doctrine. The South, according to the Senator, has the wealth, as evinced by its exports: the North has built the ships, and has very far transcended the South in all kinds of industrial and commercial enterprises. The South has, we cannot but remark, been very much misunderstood, if its people do not generally consume their income. It is commonly believed that a very great majority of the planters spend their income before their cotton has reached its final market. Before the fact of exportation can be admitted as proof of Southern wealth, it should be known by whom it is exported, how much was sold before shipment and to whom, how much mortgaged and to what extent. Accurate information on these points might reveal the curious fact, that the North exports the cotton, and that it is a Northern surplus which goes to Europe in the shape of cotton-bales. The Five Cotton States are large importers of Northern commodities, many of which are made expressly for them; in payment for these, and for advances on cotton, they give not their surplus of cotton, but the chief part of their cotton, either in kind, or in Bills of Exchange drawn upon it, or Bills of Lading transferring the ownership of it.

This by way of suggestion to the Senator, lest he provoke more particular researches into the question, Who exports the cotton? Be that as it may, it is susceptible of very clear proof, that the Five Cotton States spend their entire annual income. The facts and considerations already adduced show this; but no such unfavorable inferences need be drawn from this expenditure as those made by the Senator. It is no matter of reproach, nor proof of poverty, to spend an income; the question is, How is it spent?

THE INCOME OF THE EIGHT STATES—HOW IT IS SPENT.

We do not deny the allegation of the Senator, that at the North we spend every year our vast income; nor is there much objection to disclose how we spend it. The North has now twenty millions of people, who expend, on the average, for clothing, furniture, and house-rent, $50 for each person. That consumes about a thousand millions of dollars of their income: of this only about ten or twelve dollars for each is imported, which imposes a tax of about two dollars each. The North has, in the last fifty years, made a huge investment in houses, factories, and the improvement of estates in land. In the eight States mentioned as being near to New York, and as covering 128,000 square miles, the cities of New York and Brooklyn have been built with their 86,000 houses, the city of Philadelphia with its 89,000 houses, the cities of Baltimore and Boston with their 80,000 houses — the furnaces, foundries, machine-shops, the woollen and cotton factories, and other manufacturing establishments — having cost at least two thousand millions, but worth to-day not more than fifteen hundred millions. The heaviest investment made by the eight States, however, is in the improvement of their lands, of which they own 128,000 square miles, upon which a vast amount of labor and money has been expended in buildings, drainage, fencing, and improving the soil, so that it is now fairly worth an average of $30 per acre, or $20,000 a square mile.

A large amount of Northern savings has been invested in shipping, and in sea and river steamers, of which the capacity is stated in the Treasury Reports at upwards of one million of tons. This cost a vast sum more; it is safe to place the value now at fifty millions.

These eight States have constructed 9,000 miles of railway, and 2500 miles of canals, which cost above $25,000 per mile, and may be put down as worth at least $20,000, or, altogether, $230,000,000.

Many other important items of Northern wealth, developed and made available by Northern capital and Northern labor, might be added, such as mines of coal, iron, and other metals, the annual crop of ice, etc. ; but we have stated enough to show that if, at the North, we consume our income, we have something to show for the consumption.

Investments of the States of Massachusetts, Connecticut, Rhode Island, New York, New Jersey, Pennsylvania, Delaware, and Maryland, with an estimated population of ten millions.

For Clothing and Furniture (annual)..................	$500,000,000
New York and Brooklyn, 86,000 houses at $6000...	516,000,000
Philadelphia, 89,000 houses at $4000.................	356,000,000
Baltimore and Boston, 80,000 houses at $4000......	320,000,000
Factories, Furnaces, Machinery of every kind.........	1,500,000,000
Land, 128,000 square miles at $20,000...............	2,867,200,000
Shipping and Steamers of the eight States............	40,000,000
Railroads, 9000 miles — Canals, 2500 miles...........	230,000,000
	$6,329,200,000

In the five Cotton States their population is eighteen to the square mile, in the eight States it is eighty; in the first, the land is worth on the average five dollars, and thirty dollars in the other. In the five States there is a mile of railroad or canal for every eighty square miles of territory; in the eight, there is one for every eleven square miles. Both North and South, the system of agriculture has been very far from what it should be; but the Southern system has proved the worst. By the census of 1850, Southern lands were valued at six dollars the acre; in the eight States named, at over thirty-five dollars. If the 2,060,000 of white population in the five States consume to the value of fifty dollars in clothing and furniture for each person, amounting to over one hundred millions of dollars, we cannot understand how they pay for it — for their surplus for all purposes, except food, is less than sixty millions, and probably not exceeding fifty millions. But we forbear to follow this contrast, and hope that those who are most concerned will do it for themselves, and be stimulated to study their true economical interests in the light of the "trashy census-books," rather than under the inspiration of the wild conjectures and egregious errors of Senator Hammond. The census-books, whatever be their imperfections, are safer guides than the figures or the fancies of Senator Hammond's Speech.

It would not have been worth while to follow the Senator of South Carolina in his mistaken statements and ill-considered conclusions, if we had not known they were entertained by multitudes who are, at this moment, inspired by them in their rash and thoughtless efforts to break away from a government and confederacy from which, if they have not derived all the benefits they ought to have enjoyed, it is chiefly their own fault. The Union of the States, by bringing a larger territory and a more widely diffused people under one government, no doubt made it absolutely necessary to study and work out new problems of labor and social economy. Instead of doing this, to the extent it has been done at the North, the five Cotton States have betaken themselves to the single industrial occupation of planting, and to the single political occupation of party politics. Having neglected to make the most of a very advantageous position, they are now

making gigantic efforts to change that position, and
achieve one full of danger, and only to be maintained at
continuous risk and enormous expense. One-half the expenditure to be incurred in attaining an independent position, and making it secure, would place these States in
the Union in a position both of power and wealth, from
which they would have no wish to escape.

OTHER SPECIMENS OF THE SENATOR'S SPEECH.

The Senator plumes himself exceedingly upon the immense production of the South: "If I am right in my
calculation of $220,000,000 of surplus produce, there is
not a nation on the face of the earth, with any numerous
population, that can compete with us in produce *per
capita*. It amounts to $16.66 per head, supposing that we
have 12,000,000 of people. England, with all her accumulated wealth and concentrated energy, makes but $16 of
surplus production per head." In the estimate of the five
Cotton States, we have allowed for an export of cotton,
producing $29 for each person, which makes the Senator's
argument stronger. An income of $29 for each person does
not make a people rich, even if they are provided with
food. If these States were producing commodities consumed at home to the extent of $20 each, and exported to
the amount of $29 each, it would afford evidence of
wealth. But they export nearly their entire product,
which is cotton only, giving them $29 each, out of which
they have to pay $16 each for the expense of producing
their cotton, leaving only $13 for all other purposes to
each person, or $55,000,000 altogether. The reference of
the Senator to England is not a happy one. The products
of the industry of the United Kingdom, besides those of
agriculture, upon which they rely for food, is not less than
£280,000,000, or about £10 for each person. If the foreign
trade of the United Kingdom earns enough to pay for the
raw material of the British manufacturers, which may be

the case, the British and Irish people enjoy an average income of $50 for each person, besides so much of their food as is derived from their own soil: whilst the highest net income the five Cotton States can justly claim for each individual is $13 upon the whole population, and about $27 for the whites.

Upon the principle of the Senator, the planters who make sugar and the manufacturers who make iron can have no surplus, for they export nothing; or, if he admits the idea of domestic exports, then his doctrine is, that all the sugar and iron sold is surplus production. But both these classes of men would be slow to admit, as a fact, that their whole product, if sold, was their surplus. Those persons in the Cotton States who are of the Senator's way of thinking, have, it is feared, lost sight of the fact, that the expense of production must be paid, before a surplus can be realized or a dividend made. With $13 for each individual, after paying the expense of making and placing their cotton in market, the Senator should be cautious in proclaiming the South to be the most productive region "on the face of the earth"!

THE SENATOR'S ESTIMATE OF THE REVENUE, SOUTH.

"With an export of $220,000,000," the Senator remarks, "under the present tariff, the South, organized separately, would have $40,000,000 of revenue." Even if the South had commodities to that value to export, it cannot export them without help from some quarter: it must sell a large portion, and receive heavy advances on the remainder. The South cannot, by any possibility, for twenty years to come, pay for foreign commodities enough to raise forty millions of revenue under the duties imposed by the present tariff: there is no escape on the part of the South from the dire necessity of paying for the production of the two hundred millions' worth of home commodities which would be sent to pay for the two hundred millions' worth

of foreign goods upon which that amount of revenue could
be levied. For, though slaves work without wages, the
expense of their clothes, medical attendance, overseers,
hospitals, houses, furniture, &c., involves a large outlay.
The South could not purchase that quantity of goods,
because the people have not now, and never had, the
means to pay for them. We believe the South does not
in any year purchase and pay for forty millions' worth of
foreign commodities; nor does the desire exist there
to consume two hundred millions' worth of foreign goods.
If there did not exist the least obstacle in the way of
duties upon imports, the South, it is believed, would purchase the largest portion of her supplies from the North,
and especially agricultural implements, all kinds of vehicles
upon wheels from the finest carriages for pleasure to the
coarsest and strongest carts and wheelbarrows, wooden
furniture, and cabinet work. The foreign freight on such
articles would equal a heavy duty. Besides, the same
universal facilities for credit could not be obtained in
Europe as in the North. The people living in neighboring
countries in Europe do not give to each other any such
credit as the Northern cities give to Southern merchants.
They could only obtain credit at a banker's upon a deposit
of cotton. Imagine that Southern merchants and planters
enjoyed no other credit than what they could obtain upon
cotton in Liverpool or Havre. They have heretofore
obtained either the whole money, or a heavy advance,
before the cotton left the American port; in addition to
which the Southern merchant, through whom the planters
receive their supplies, obtains a credit in New York and
other Northern cities of eight to twelve months for his
purchases, which enables him to extend a like credit or
a still longer one to the planters. This system gives the
planters one entire year of credit, or, in other words,
capital for a year's business one year in advance. No
such credit as this can be established with European merchants. It is contrary to all their usages and ideas of safe
methods of trade.

"THE SOUTH WOULD NEVER GO TO WAR"—"NEVER DREAM OF WAR."

"The South," says the Senator, "would never go to war. It is commerce that breeds war. It is manufactures, that require to be hawked about the world, that give rise to navies and commerce." What a tranquil, inoffensive people are they of the South! They resort to arms! No: only do as they tell you, hold your tongue, and have no opinion about any thing where Slavery is concerned, and you need not fear their pistols, knives, or canes!—We leave this remarkable opinion or prophecy of the wise Senator to the men of the South who are shouting defiance to the United States, and stand bristling with arms.

"But we have nothing to do," he continues, "but to take off restrictions upon foreign merchandise and open our ports, and the whole world will come to us to trade." The "whole world" is not likely to be in the least degree excited by the prospect of free access to less than ten millions of people, of whom half are African slaves. Two hundred millions of dollars' worth of cotton, upon which the holders want an advance of one hundred and fifty millions in money, will make but a small ripple on the surface of the world's commerce. The South has never exported but a small portion of her own products, and can never become an exporter to any extent of the products of the North. The ports of the South are not surrounded with such a population as can afford basis for any considerable trade; nor is that population, such as it is, so occupied as to uphold a large trade. The South does not build up cities or towns, and cannot have a great foreign trade, because she has not the consumers; and it can invite foreign trade only to the extent the people have the means of buying. The whole products of the South, even if they could be all expended in foreign products, would

not build up a Baltimore, much less a New York. There
are many Free Ports, or ports where the duties are merely
nominal, in Europe, such as Hamburg, Bremen, Lubec,
Genoa, and Leghorn, each one of which is surrounded
with a population of ten millions of free whites in the
same space where there is one million of free and slave
in the South. Not one of these Free Ports has a population or wealth equal to the City of Boston. The system
of industry adopted by the South forbids the growth of '
cities and the increase of free population. No offers which
the South can make to the commercial world will tempt
the world's agents to leave their chosen channels of trade,
and come to the four ports of the South for two hundred
millions of dollars' worth of cotton. It is a vast and
varied industry which begets a great exchange of commodities and builds cities. Those of Great Britain only
commenced their growth when the manufacturing career
of that country began. Irish cities do not grow; nor does
Ireland increase in wealth, as England and Scotland.

"WITHOUT FIRING A GUN"—"THE WHOLE WORLD AT OUR FEET."

" Without firing a gun, without drawing a sword, should
they make war upon us, we could bring the whole world
to our feet." The South, according to the Senator, is
nearly omnipotent. It needs only open its doors, and the
whole world must come thither to trade and get their
share of cotton; but if the world disputes the will of the
South, it will be brought to a speedy and deep humiliation—to the very feet of the South—Asia, Africa, Europe,
South America, and the British Dominions in the North,
with New York, Pennsylvania, and the great West, at the
feet of the South! Within two years after this bravado
the South is as busy with guns as ever she was with
cotton. The money to be now spent in war would more
than establish a system of industry in the South which

would open up a career of prosperity tenfold what any system of free ports could ever attain.

"The South is perfectly competent to go on one, two, or three years, without planting a seed of cotton." That will be news to many planters of cotton, and will appear very striking intelligence to a large number of dealers with the South, who have been under the impression that a great majority of the planters spend each year's income .before the cotton is sold.

"What would happen, if no cotton was furnished for three years?" . . . "England would topple headlong, and carry the whole civilized world with her. No, you dare not make war upon cotton. No power on earth dares to make war upon it. Cotton is king. Until lately, the Bank of England was king; but she tried to put her screws, as usual, the fall before the last, on the cotton crop, and was utterly vanquished. The last power has been conquered. Who can doubt, that has looked at recent events, that cotton is supreme?" This is the kind of gas which propels the wheels of revolution in South Carolina. It has been forced into the people of Charleston with such success, that the whole city is now in a flame, which must blaze as long as the gas is supplied. These utterances are too mighty for human nature to hear and be tranquil; even the great Southern agriculturists, who never "dream of war," who are as innocent as they are rich, have become perfectly intoxicated with their power and the grandeur of King Cotton, who, having vanquished the Bank of England and President Buchanan, is now considering what he will do with New York and the North.

To be serious: has not many a man ended his days in an insane hospital, who never uttered any thing more absurd than this speech? It could not justify a moment's consideration, if the same egregious folly had not taken possession of a school of Southern politicians, who, under the impulse of this madness, are striving, with madmen's strength, to pull down the pillars of that Constitution

4

which has been the chief bulwark of their social system, and the foundation of its success, so far as Slavery is concerned.

POLITICAL FREEDOM — FREEDOM OF SPEECH.

We did not intend to follow the Senator further; but, believing it will be a safe rule to travel in a direction opposite to that which he takes, we quote another of his opinions, to make it the text of some remarks intended to support a very different doctrine. " The greatest strength of the South arises from the harmony of her political and social institutions. This harmony gives her a frame of society, the best in the world, and an extent of political freedom, combined with entire security, such as no other people ever enjoyed upon the face of the earth." Upon all the points taken here, there are many who would differ strongly from the Senator. The special topic to which we would draw the attention of the reader is, the "political freedom" here made a matter of boast.

Slavery is held by the leading politicians in the South, and a large class of the leading men who are not politicians, to be an institution not only defensible, but commendable in every respect, and, so far as labor is concerned, every way preferable to our Northern system of labor for wages. It is not our object to discuss the subject of Slavery now, nor to give any opinion about it, in a moral point of view, further than to say that between the master and his African slave the duty of each is to do for the other the best that is in his power. The slave being brought from savage life needs to be inured to habits of labor, to be taught various branches of industry, to be civilized and prepared for freedom when the time arrives, that emancipation may improve his condition. Freedom without due preparation for the change it involves, both in the position of the slave and in the society to which he belongs, would sink the race emancipated to an immea-

surably worse condition than Slavery as it now exists in
our country. The presence of slaves thus emancipated
would be intolerable; they would become the criminals,
vagabonds, paupers, and outcasts of our present civiliza-
tion. We look upon the Southern masters as men having
the heavy responsibility of these slaves cast upon them, as
bound to study the best interests of their people in con-
nection with the interests of society and the whole country, but as accountable for the discharge of their duties in
this behalf only to their own consciences, to the laws of
their own States, and to God. We regard African Slavery, as now existing in the South, as justifiable upon
sound, social, humane, and Christian considerations. We
would justify no abuse, nor be understood to say that the
system should not be amended: we mean merely the relation of master and slave. This was the opinion and the
feeling of the leading minds of this country at the time
our Constitution was adopted. They desired to see an
end of Slavery, but did not undertake to prescribe how
that end should be accomplished. That was left to the
owners of slaves.

As a large majority of those who hold slaves in the
South entertain much stronger opinions in favor of Slavery now than were then prevalent, nothing pertaining to
the subject has surprised us more, or caused greater
anxiety for the future, than the position generally taken
by them in reference to the discussion of the subject.
They maintain that Slavery is a beneficial institution —
best for the master, best for the slave, best for society;
they believe that it furnishes a "frame of society the best
on the face of the earth"; they declare that society so
constituted is not only preferable to that of the other
States where Slavery does not exist, but they insist that
society without Slavery, in the United States, is a failure;
yet they permit no discussion, they tolerate no shades of a
different opinion, they permit not the slightest expression
of dissent; they have not only taken away the right of

free speech, but have established a despotism over the minds
and the utterance of the people constituting that superior
society, which has no parallel in the civilized world. If
this despotism, or any thing approaching it, were necessary, some justification might be pleaded for an exercise
of power, which not only shuts the mouth, but crushes the
mind and manliness of all who are its victims. For fifty
years, and more, after this government was constituted,
the subject of Slavery was as freely and publicly discussed
and talked about, and was the object of as many different
opinions, as any other great topic. It was discussed in
the North as occasion required; and in the South, in public conventions, in Legislatures with reference to the Colo-
nization Society, with reference to gradual emancipation,
and the merits of Slavery were often earnestly called in
question: through all this, for half a century, Slavery flourished, and no man can point to any evil resulting from
this free speech that can compare with one hour of the
savage and watchful despotism enforced for some years
past in parts of the Southern States. It is a mistake to
suppose that this tyranny of politicians and their servant,
the mob, can be approved by the best people in the South;
it is abhorred, and only submitted to for sake of quiet,
and in the hope that it will be of short duration. If Slavery had not another enemy in the world, not another in-
fluence working its downfall, this despotism would accomplish it. Who of his neighbors, if a freeman lives in the
South, is to decide what he may or may not say? The
Constitution guarantees the right of trial by jury in crimi-
nal cases, and in cases of civil dispute; but he who, in the
South, expresses an opinion in regard to Slavery distaste-
ful to his hearers, is liable to be seized, imprisoned, beaten,
tarred and feathered, and banished, if not hung on the
spot, without trial, judge, or jury. Nay, all this may occur
to a man who has not breathed a word about Slavery, if
he only be supposed to come from a place where men
speak their minds.

In many parts of the South, this zeal for the repression of free speech has been worked up to a blind rage, which smacks strongly of insanity, and the people who indulge in it have assumed an attitude so defiant, so fierce and vigilant, as to suggest that the whole South is but a magazine of gun-cotton, ready to explode at the word, or even look of a man from the North, or the frank expression of an opinion by a man of the South. If every slave were made of powder, and liable to go off at a word, these repressionists could not be more on their guard, and more ready to pounce upon free speech. They behave as if the very existence of Slavery, and the entire fabric of Southern society, depended upon silence like death. If the ghosts of all the Africans who have been smothered in the middle passage — of all who have been thrown overboard to escape capture — and of all who have died in Slavery — were now besetting these champions of Slavery with all the terrors of pandemonium, they could not stand more aghast than they do at the appearance of an abolitionist, or of a man who may be an abolitionist, or of a man of the South who utters a word not deemed by them orthodox on the subject of Slavery.

Now, whatever be the language of the abolitionists, however provoking, however inexcusable both in a social and Christian point of view, their chief power to do any mischief has arisen from the importance given to them by the notice taken of their proceedings, in the South. If the South has confidence in its view of Slavery, why listen to or resent the ravings of men whose minds are so badly adjusted? To be so strongly affected by the presence or language of abolitionists, argues a similar want of balance. There has been no President, from Washington to Buchanan, who has not been denounced as guilty of sins as great as those charged on the slaveholders. The great factions which have struggled for possession of the government of this country have denounced each other, in mass and as individuals, as guilty of crimes of the blackest dye;

there are few monarchs of Europe, or conspicuous public
men, who do not receive and endure an equal share of
abuse. The priests, and the clergy, and professing Chris-
tians, have not been spared — for the cohorts of infidelity
are still more numerous than those of the abolitionists.

Why, then, of all the men who are well abused, should
the slaveholder and his champions exhibit the least self-
respect, the least patience and power of endurance? The
writers and orators of the South are no strangers to the
task of evil speaking — they have shown themselves capable of pouring out floods of abuse, when occasion offered.
They should have learned, ere now, to take as well as
give. It was a fatal mistake to refuse the petitions of the
abolitionists; that policy increased their numbers and
boldness. It is, to this day, the corner-stone of their
power; for many who detested their course and doctrines
thought the petitions should have been received, and then
condemned. They are encouraged in their work by see-
ing that, if they can do nothing else, they are able to stir
up a great deal of ire; that, if they cannot touch the heart
of the slaveholder, they can at least stir up gall, and pierce
the fountains of bitterness. The abolitionists have lived
upon notoriety, which they could not have achieved but
by the help of the impatient and rash defenders of Slavery. Let them alone; they will yet sink into the insig-
nificance to which, by their numbers, they belong. They
are alike the enemies of Slavery and the Constitution of
their country, and not a few of them, of the Bible. Doubtless there are many in the North who do not hold the
same opinion of Slavery as the men of the South, but they
are neither the enemies of the master, nor of their country; they will abide by the Constitution and its proper
interpreters; and if their brethren of the South should
ever, in a time of danger, need their assistance, it would
be given with promptness and efficiency. They do not
differ in opinion from slaveholders, on the subject of Slavery, more than the prevailing parties differ upon other

topics. That difference should be endured, even upon the delicate subject of Slavery; it is so inevitable, that it exists among slaveholders themselves, who freely expressed very diverse opinions as long as they were permitted to give vent to their thoughts. Let that freedom be speedily restored, and let no man hereafter assume to determine what his neighbor may say; let the important right of free speech be only under the curb of the law, and the duly constituted tribunals of justice.

A CONFERENCE OF SLAVE-OWNERS.

It is quite certain that Slavery in the South is not understood and appreciated at the North or in Europe as it should be, and it is scarcely less certain that it is not universally understood at the South as it should be. An institution which so much concerns the interests and well-fare of human beings, for this life and the life to come, deserves to be continuously studied. Many able, learned, and valuable works on the subject of Slavery have come to us from the South; we have yet, however, to receive from that quarter a great and authoritative exposition of the institution — not in the shape of a defence, nor of an apology, but of a social exposition, in which Slavery, as it exists at the South, shall be fully and ably presented, in its aspects, historical and actual: in its relations with society; the relations of master and servant; the family relations of the negroes; the sale and transfer of negroes; the property in negroes, and the various consequences of that relation; the degree and kind of education, religious and otherwise, to be given to the negro, and all that concerns the industrial and economical aspects of the institution, both now and in the future. Slavery deserves a social code of its own, co-extensive with the Slave States. There are many large slaveholders of the South so intelligent, so well-prepared by experience and long reflection, so full of sympathy for the slaves and the desire to do the

best for them that can be devised, that, if brought together
for conference, they could produce a series of invaluable
papers, presenting the whole subject in a form alike important to master and slave, to South and North, and to
the whole nation. This might lead to a constitution for
Slavery, a slave code for the Slave States, and a uniform
social policy respecting the management of slaves. We
have scarce ever heard any thing with more interest than
the accounts we have received from Southern planters of
the social and economical policy pursued on their plantations. A convention, such as we suggest, would bring to
the public eye the best results of thousands of well-devised
and fairly-tried experiments. Such an assemblage, for such
a purpose, would be an honor to the South, an honor to
the public institutions of the United States; it would go
very far to remove ignorance and unfavorable opinions in
the North and in Europe. After such a measure, well carried out, abolitionism could no longer flourish; the occupation would be no longer profitable; its leaders would be
under the necessity of seeking employment more conso-
nant with Christian kindness and the peace of society.
And others of the North who now regard Slavery with a
distrustful and hopeless feeling, would begin to look upon
it as a sure method of elevating the African from savage
to civilized life, and to give the master words of cheer,
instead of undissembled distrust.

There is a class of slaveholders in the South who may
not receive suggestions of this kind in good part, especially in moments of excitement. There is another,
however, who will welcome any thing that is well intended, and give it as much consideration as it may
appear to deserve. To such we address ourselves, and
desire them, when the present excitement is past, end as
it may, to consider, whether a meeting of fifty or a hundred slave-owners could not do something to improve the
institution of Slavery, and make it better for the master
and better for the man. Slavery, like every other human

institution, is susceptible of progress in the right direction. There is a wide interval between Slavery as established on some plantations and as seen on others. Let the best and, most successful methods be brought to light and set up as guides for others, and let the united wisdom and experience of slaveholders be brought to bear on the whole subject. Let it become a study, as much as the science of legislation or government.

Slavery is a great institution. It concerns, in this country, the interests of four millions of people, who, from the necessity of the case, can have no voice in determining their own condition. History has fully warned us, that emancipations of slaves on a large scale are hazardous experiments, which, in most cases, have failed in ameliorating the condition of those to whom freedom is given in this manner. No adequate preparation can be made for wholesale emancipation. Slaves set free in large numbers rapidly sink to the condition of criminals and vagabonds. There have been many instances of this. So it was with the emancipations in the early years of Christianity. So it was with the feudal emancipations of England; and so it is with the British emancipation, and with that of the French West Indies in 1848. St. Domingo, where the slaves took their freedom, is far from proving any thing in favor of wholesale emancipation.

This door being shut, we are led to inquire, Whether Slavery is not capable of elevating itself; Whether slaves cannot work out their own emancipation; and Whether any other mode of emancipation, where large numbers are concerned, is practicable or beneficial to slaves, than that which sets freedom before them as the reward of a course of industry distinctly marked out. The present system in the South makes no provision for increase of white population; if that system is continued, another should be adopted, by which, within a hundred years, the negroes should purchase not only themselves, but the lands of their masters. When the negroes shall have

done this, their freedom may be safely conferred, because
they will be able to maintain it; when they, by their own
labor, pay for themselves, under a system arranged by
the masters, they will have become thrifty enough to
make their way in the world.   It may take a long time
for such a system to accomplish an end of Slavery.   Very
true : it may require generations, but it will prevent undue increase, while it takes nothing from the masters ;
and will send forth very few freedmen of the class who
become nuisances to the community in which they reside.

    We think it not only right, but indispensable, that the
slave-owners of the South should look at the subject in
regard to its future ; for if they make no provision for the
time when there will be twenty millions of slaves, where
there are now only four millions, the white inhabitants
will either forsake several States, or be driven from them.
The whites and blacks cannot inhabit the same States in
the disproportion which will then exist.   It is morally and
socially impossible ; it is economically impossible that
South Carolina could hold in peace and comfort a million
of blacks and a third of a million of whites.   This may be
the case in less than forty years ; and in less than ten
years the price of cotton will fall, because a competition
will be established, by the untiring efforts of English capitalists, against the planters of this country, in India, China,
Africa, in Central and in parts of South America.   This
will enable the purchasers of cotton better to control the
market of this country, by playing all the rest against it.
Cotton will not only come down in price, but negroes will
come down, because there will be an over-supply ; cotton
will not pay as it does now, and the slaves will eat their
masters out of house and home.   No rate of dispersion in
new States can so moderate the increase of slaves as mate-
rially to postpone that conjunction of events which will
produce the alternative of a separation between master and
slave — the master must desert his post, or the slaves will
drive him away.   The dispersion by sales and emigration

must cease when slave-labor fails to be profitable, as will
be the case, so far as cotton is concerned, in less than ten
years. It is well known that this over-supply of slave-
labor now exists in Eastern Virginia, and that, but for the
outlet afforded in States further south, owing to the high
price of cotton, Virginia and South Carolina would, at
this moment, be overwhelmed with an over-population of
negroes. The purchase of Louisiana saved them. The
emigration to the Gulf States, and to the valley of the
Mississippi, of the planters with their slaves, the sale of
an immense number every year by the owners still remaining, postponed an evil, which is yet inevitable, unless provided against in time. Nothing like the acquisition of
Louisiana can again occur in the history of the country;
and if it could, it needs only a reduction in the price of
cotton to make it nugatory as a preventive of the evil of
over-population. There is yet south of the Missouri Com-
promise Line a vast cotton territory, but it is occupied
slowly; and cotton will be down, and the dispersion will
cease, long before it can be occupied. The evil will then
rapidly supervene in many of the States, of having one
hundred slaves to feed and clothe where fifty only are
wanted. The slaves cannot be sold, though they make
the land worthless, for they must consume its whole product. This dire calamity impends equally in the Union
or out of it. The nature of it is well known, both in Virginia and South Carolina; and sad results were beginning
to be felt, when succor came in the shape of high prices.
Prices fluctuate, but the tendency is steadily downward.
The present high prices of cotton are producing their
usual effect — competition is growing up all over the
world. It will be felt in the South in three years; it will
produce suffering in less than seven years.

Now is the time to act: every expedient which the wit
of man can devise should be put in operation to provide
adequately against the approaching evil — an evil which
our children may live to see, and feel, and deplore. How

much time shall be lost in squabbling over political abstractions? How much in struggles for political power, which demoralize all who are engaged in them? Let the prudent owners of slaves look forward beyond these temporary affairs, at what is to be the condition of their estates ten, twenty, or thirty years hence. We say again, then, that the wisest and best men of the South should get together, men free from every taint of party demoralization, as soon as practicable, and examine the whole subject of Slavery in its present condition and future prospects. Slavery deserves to be studied and treated far above the atmosphere of opposing factions and selfish partisans.

If Slavery is to be permanent, as is contemplated by the South, there is the more reason why those concerned, as owners and residents, should give themselves to the earnest study of it as a social institution, destined, before half a century, to deal with twenty millions of slaves. But Slavery cannot be permanent unless the masters can secure freedom of speech and a tranquil life, though surrounded by neighbors who do not appreciate the institution, or who may dislike it.

SECURITY FROM INSURRECTION AND FROM INVASION.

There is a topic upon which we shall now venture a few remarks, well knowing that some will not regard them as timely, and that others will look upon it as presumption, to advise those who know best. In the hope that we may stimulate those who know best to give special attention to one matter which has not been, as we believe, well considered, we submit our suggestions. We refer to security from insurrection and invasion, and to the safety of families from the attack of slaves. It appears to us there is less harmony of opinion and practice, on this subject, than there should be on one of such vital importance. A conference, such as we have proposed, would look upon this as one of the first topics which should engage its attention. Such a conference would certainly embrace many persons who would fully understand what we wish to say, and who could say it much better. The main element of safety is in the character of the African and his American descendants. These people are, by nature, kind, affectionate, and faithful; the very fact that, in such a country, on such a frontier of Slave States, there have not been more fugitives, exhibits the faithful and quiet disposition of the slaves, and certifies strongly to kind treatment by the masters. It is not in the least probable that slaves who will not run from their masters, will think of murder or insurrection. There has never been as many murders of white people by blacks in the South, in proportion to population, as of whites by whites in the North. Thousands of most touching instances of faithfulness and attachment to masters have been recorded, but the tithe of these cases has never been made public. It is not necessary to tell the slave-owner that kindness and justice to his slaves is his best security; he knows that, and his compliance with this duty is fully attested by the history of American Slavery, where even the symptoms of insurrection have been so rare, and where the great increase of the population proves they have been neither overworked nor underfed, nor have they suffered by neglect. The history of Slavery in Cuba, and in the British West Indies, exhibits a fearfully different result. There is, at this time, in the South fifteen times as many negroes as were ever imported — in the West Indies there are not now, it is believed, three times as many. The American master has been kind and considerate as to the health and comfort of his slaves; and he has his reward in the superior strength, constitution, and intelligence of his slaves. The value of their labor is in the same proportion.

But something more than this general kindness is required in a matter which concerns not only life and property, but the very existence of society. For one cruel and bad managing master, among fifty of a different kind, may drive hundreds of slaves to desperation, and bring danger upon those who had done nothing to provoke it. The truth is, that there is more to fear from imprudent and bad masters, than there is from the negroes, when as well treated as they are, for the most part. No statutes could be framed which would cover adequately cases of this kind; nothing short of a regular organization of the slave-owners, as extensive, if possible, as Slavery, with the view of establishing a code of treatment. These organizations might for convenience be connected with county agricultural societies, a county court, or any other periodical assemblage. Among the chief men of a county it would not be difficult to have an understanding, what was and what was not right and safe in the management of slaves. The public opinion generated by this association would be perhaps sufficient to curb the most of those who would offend. The mode of restraining those whose bad passions or rashness public opinion could not control would belong to the assembled wisdom of the county.

We suggest this organization only to make way for another which we regard as far more important, and that is a regular police, selected from the slaves, of such numbers and for such specified duties as each locality might make necessary. The slave population throughout the South would furnish men as reliable and as fit for this duty as need be desired. Two or three per cent., at most five per cent., of those above eighteen years of age would suffice for this purpose, which would not involve, ordinarily, absence from labor one whole day in a month. It is well known how dependent large cities are for protection upon the police. It is notorious, however, that this protection is often due in part to bad men, who contrive to procure positions in the police for the purpose of occasionally making common cause with thieves and other criminals. With all this, the police of our cities, at times badly tainted with this class, is far better than none. Now we venture to say that an experienced police-officer, with the aid of the masters and a few experienced overseers, would organize a black police upon a system, applicable to the whole slave region, which would be an adequate protection against insurrection and against all other outbreaks of the slaves, except those due to the sudden impulses of passion.

The members of this black police would appear once a month or oftener before their chief, a white man, to make their verbal report, and receive instructions. The full significancy of their position need not be disclosed to them. It would be enough for them to know, that they were to look out for all bad negroes and bad white men who might be found lurking in the neighborhood, and to keep their ears wide open to all the gossip that might concern their masters. If they were dubbed with the title of Captains, it would add to their vigilance. There would seldom be any occasion for their traversing their districts, and care would be necessary that they should not incur the odium which belongs to spies and informers. We assume that the slave would be proud of his office — faithful, because that is his character—pleased with the rewards and notice he would receive. Where many were found suitable, they might be changed, and the office given in rotation or as a reward of good conduct. It would require, of course, some time for such a system to become fully understood and to receive the exact form in which it would work best. Whether they should assemble once a month or once in three months, with a proper uniform, for drill and a good dinner; whether they should be taught the use of arms; whether they should have a staff or any thing else to exhibit on occasion as their badge of office, would be considerations for those who would have the chief supervision.

We forbear to enlarge upon this suggestion; if it meets with any favor from those who are most interested, they will find no difficulty in obtaining valuable hints from police officers of skill and experience in New York and Philadelphia and elsewhere. Having the firm belief, that there are among the slaves enough of the faithful to afford ample and sure protection to the masters, we offer the above as a mode of attaining it. Out of this danger, if it exists, the people of the South can pluck safety,—a safety so complete as to defy all the Abolitionists and John Browns in the country. We believe no city in the world could have a more faithful police than the masters can select from their slaves. In time it might be made the means of forming a military force of great strength and fidelity.

We should not have presumed to make this suggestion, but for the apprehensions now existing in the South; but for that terror which has been created and is now maintained by the enemies of the Union or by mere politicians, whose artifice has been to swell their party and keep up its discipline by playing on the fears of their constituents, and creating a constant dread of inroads by Abolitionists or insurrection of slaves.

If there is any ground for the present terror, for the present fear of Abolitionists, for that despotic prohibition of free speech now prevailing in portions of the South, which we do not believe, there is good reason for considering some such plan of safety as we propose. We beg the people of the South to believe, that there is not an Abolitionist in New England or in New York who would head an insurrection in any part of the Slave States. John Brown and his associates were educated for their crime in Kansas. It was in civil war, the most terrible and demoralizing of all wars, that he and they were prepared for the villany of Harper's Ferry. If we are now unhappily on the eve of that greatest of human calamities, a civil war, there cannot be a doubt the South will be pierced in a thousand places; and insurrection, with fire and sword, will be carried into thousands upon thousands of homes that were lately happy — homes that might be still among the happiest on earth, but for the treachery of politicians and the treason of men in high places.

THE END.